SAMURAI

SAMURAI

JEANNE NAGLE

Britannica
Educational Publishing

Published in 2017 by Britannica Educational Publishing (a trademark of Encyclopædia Britannica, Inc.) in association with The Rosen Publishing Group, Inc.
29 East 21st Street, New York, NY 10010

Distributed exclusively by Rosen Publishing.
To see additional Britannica Educational Publishing titles, go to rosenpublishing.com.

First Edition

Britannica Educational Publishing
J.E. Luebering: Executive Director, Core Editorial
Anthony L. Green: Editor, Compton's by Britannica

Rosen Publishing
Heather Moore Niver: Editor
Nelson Sá: Creative Director
Matt Cauli: Designer
Cindy Reiman: Photography Manager
Heather Moore Niver: Photo Researcher

Library of Congress Cataloging-in-Publication Data

Names: Nagle, Jeanne, author.
Title: Samurai / Jeanne Nagle.
Description: New York : Britannica Educational Publishing, in association
 with Rosen Educational Services, [2017] | Series: Warriors around the
 world | Includes bibliographical references and index. | Audience: Grades
 5–8.
Identifiers: LCCN 2016020480 | ISBN 9781508103721 (library bound : alk. paper)
 | ISBN 9781508104322 (pbk. : alk. paper) | ISBN 9781508102984 (6-pack :
 alk. paper)
Subjects: LCSH: Samurai—History—Juvenile literature. | Japan—History—To
 1868—Juvenile literature.
Classification: LCC DS827.S3 N32 2016 | DDC 952/.025—dc23
LC record available at https://lccn.loc.gov/2016020480

Manufactured in China

Photo credits: Cover, p. 3 (samurai) Volodymyr Krasyuk/Shutterstock.com; cover, p. 3 (background) Luciano Mortula/Shutterstock.com; pp. 7, 21 Bettmann/Getty Images; p. 9 Library of Congress, Washington, D.C.; p. 10 (inset) Culture Club/Hulton Archive/Getty Images; p. 12 John Stevenson/Corbis Historical/Getty Images; p. 14 De Agostini Picture Library/Getty Images; p. 18 Werner Forman/Universal Images Group/Getty Images; p. 19 © Photo Japan/Alamy Stock Photo; p. 20 (inset) Chronicle/Alamy Stock Photo; pp. 23, 38-39 Universal History Archive/Universal Images Group/Getty Images; pp. 26-27 DEA/A. Dagli Orti/De Agostini/Getty Images; p. 29 Indianapolis Museum of Art/Archive Photos/Getty Images; p. 30 Time Life Pictures/The LIFE Picture Collection/Getty Images; p. 31 JTB Photo/Universal Images Group/Getty Images; p. 32 © Malcolm Fairman/Alamy Stock Photo; pp. 33 (inset), 42 Pictures from History/Bridgeman Images; p. 37 Print Collector/Hulton Archive/Getty Images; p. 40 (inset) Felice Beato/Hulton Archive/Getty Images; interior pages border and background images © iStockphoto.com/RossellaApostoli (two samurai), © iStockphoto.com/&#169 Vit Kovalcik (katana), © iStockphoto.com/mihalec (swords).

CONTENTS

INTRODUCTION

For some seven hundred years—from the twelfth to the nineteeth centuries—warriors called samurai dominated the government of Japan. Although the country also had emperors during this period, real power was in the hands of the samurai.

The term "samurai" was originally used to denote aristocratic warriors (*bushi*). The word would later come to apply to all the members of the warrior class that rose to power in the twelfth century and dominated the Japanese government for centuries after.

The first samurai protected the estates of Japanese aristocrats. Gradually they gathered in or near the capital, where they served both the military needs of the government against rebellions and also as bodyguards for the great noble houses. The samurai grew increasingly powerful until, in 1185, they gained military control of all Japan. In 1192 a samurai warrior first took the title of *shogun*, making the samurai the empire's ruling class. From then until 1868 the *shoguns* ruled Japan as a type of military government.

As all good warriors are, the samurai were very disciplined. They followed an unwritten code of conduct, called Bushido, which emphasized controlling one's emotions and maintaining good moral character at all times. Above all else, the code valued loyalty, particularly with regard to the *shogun*, whom the samurai had vowed to defend and protect. In Japan, traditionally, a warrior's training emphasized archery, swordsmanship, unarmed combat, and swimming in armor. Archers used a special type of bow known as *yumi*. The samurai were perhaps best known for using a curved-

Today, they are mostly a symbol of days gone by, but there was a time when the samurai were among the most powerful and respected members of Japanese society.

blade sword called a katana. During unarmed fighting, samurai warriors relied on their training in the martial arts, which meant they engaged in hand-to-hand combat. (The word martial refers to something that is warlike or relates to soldiers.) Popular martial arts used in the heat of battle included kendo, karate, and jujitsu.

Known for their fighting strength and abilities, the samurai, as a class of people, also had a softer side. Influenced by the teachings of Zen Buddhism, the samurai were responsible for certain classic Japanese cultural arts, such as the tea ceremony and flower arranging. Each of these customs relies heavily on discipline and order, which are well-known traits of the samurai.

By the mid-nineteenth century, lower-ranking samurai were eager for societal change and anxious to create a strong Japan in the face of encroachment by Western powers. They took part in the movement that overthrew the Tokugawa shogunate in 1868. The new government, led by the emperor Meiji, stripped the samurai of their privileged status. Some samurai rose in rebellion, but the revolts were suppressed. The reign of the samurai had effectively ended.

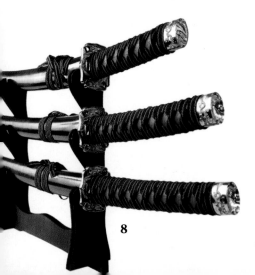

CHAPTER 1
TO BE A SAMURAI WARRIOR

Samurai warriors were skilled horsemen who could fight as well on horseback as they could with two feet on the ground.

In ancient Japan, an elaborate bureaucracy was established. At the head of this bureaucracy was the emperor, who acted as the head of state. In theory, all land belonged to the emperor. Large landholdings were abolished; some farmland was redistributed among the peasants. The government started collecting taxes on a regular basis. However, to encourage agricultural development, the government did not make people pay taxes on newly cultivated land.

This practice actually stimulated the growth of

THE RŌNIN

When a landowner died or otherwise lost his power, his samurai became masterless warriors, or rōnin. Because they no longer protected a master, the rōnin had to find either other work, which disgraced them, or a new master.

Many wound up simply wandering about the countryside, stirring up trouble among the people and employed samurai. The rōnin remained a great cause of disorder in Japan throughout the first half of the seventeenth century.

大髙源吾忠雄
近習　百石
三十二才
め

An illustration from a copy of 47 Rōnin, *the supposedly true story of a group of samurai who took revenge for their master's death.*

huge privately owned estates called *shoen*. Similar to the manors of medieval Europe, the *shoen* were owned by powerful families, court aristocrats, or religious institutions. Medieval Japanese aristocrats employed bodyguards called samurai to protect them and their landholdings. The samurai were provincial Japanese warriors who resembled medieval European knights. The samurai often managed the estates of aristocrats and sometimes held land in their own right.

RISE TO POWER

Beginning in the 1100s, the samurai warrior class rose to political power. The samurai had developed advanced military skills, and set up a military government called a shogunate. Each shogunate was headed by a *shogun*, which is the Japanese word for "general." The term used in Japan to describe the rule of a *shogun* is *bakufu*, which literally means "tent government" and suggests the field headquarters of a general while on military campaign.

As the *shoguns* acquired increased control over national affairs, they became the actual rulers of Japan. The country still had an emperor, but he held less power than the *shogun*, or military ruler. For the most part, the emperors lived mostly in seclusion and had only formal powers.

An image of Minamoto Yoritomo (center, seated), Japan's first shogun ruler, releasing cranes on a beach. Setting captured animals free is an ancient Buddhist practice.

SAMURAI AND THE THREE SHOGUNATES

There were three shogunates in Japanese history. The first was founded by Minamoto Yoritomo in 1192, known as the Kamakura shogunate. The rule of the Kamakura shogunate lasted until 1333. During this time samurai were considered warriors during wars and conflicts, but when there was peace, these men oversaw the farms owned by their lords. To keep in fighting shape, they hunted and performed martial arts training.

The second Japanese shogunate was named for the Ashikaga family, and lasted from 1338 until 1573. The Ashikaga period was a time of great military struggles. The position of the Ashikaga *shoguns* was rarely secure. They usually ruled with the cooperation of lesser warlords. Many samurai took advantage of the infighting to become *daimyo,* or land-owning warlords, themselves.

The empire's third and final shogunate was founded by Tokugawa Ieyasu. Its headquarters were at Edo (modern Tokyo), and it was in power from 1603 until 1867. It is known as either the Tokugawa or Edo shogunate. During this shogunate, a strict class structure was put into place in Japan. Even though they made up only about 7 percent of Japan's total population, the warrior class of samurai were dominant over farmers, artisans, and merchants. Eventually, though, samurai began to lose their power and their wealth. By the time the Tokugawa shogunate was nearing its end, many warriors had

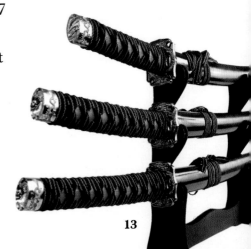

An artist's vision of Tokugawa, after whom Japan's third and final shogunate was named.

been forced to become civil servants or take other jobs in order to survive.

CODE OF CONDUCT

Starting in the medieval period, the samurai were governed by an unwritten code of conduct known as Bushido. (In Japanese,

YAMAGA SOKŌ (1622–85)

The groundwork for Bushido, the code of warriors for Japanese samurai, was laid by Yamaga Sokō, a military strategist and Confucian philosopher who also made significant contributions to the development of Japanese military science. A masterless samurai, Yamaga went to Edo, now called Tokyo, to study Buddhism, Shinto, and military tactics as well as Confucianism. In his attempts to discover standards of behavior for the samurai class, he examined the original teachings of the ancient Chinese sage Confucius. Yamaga equated the samurai with the "superior man" of Confucius. The samurai function was to keep fit for military duty and serve as an example for the lower classes.

"Bushido" means "way of the warrior.") The name Bushido was not used until the sixteenth century, but the idea of the code developed during the Kamakura period (1192–1333).

Under this code, dignity, honesty, and courage were stressed, as were frugal living, kindness, honesty, and personal honor. A samurai was expected to show affection for his family, but it was considered undignified to express his devotion outside the privacy of his home. Filial piety, which means respect and care for one's parents and other elders of the family, was also an important trait of the samurai under the code of Bushido. Above all else, however, the supreme obligation of the samurai was to his lord, even if this might cause suffering to his parents.

The precise content of the Bushido code varied historically as the samurai class came under the influence of Zen Buddhist and Confucian thought, but its one unchanging ideal was martial spirit, including athletic and military skills as well as fearlessness toward the enemy in battle.

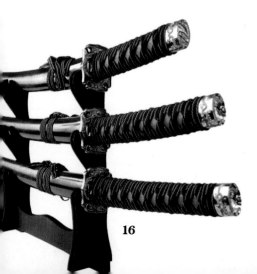

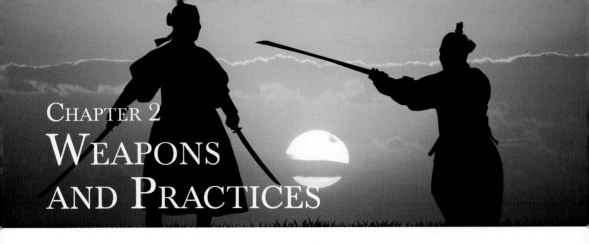

CHAPTER 2
WEAPONS AND PRACTICES

The samurai were strongly influenced by Zen Buddhism. One goal of Zen is a state of individual enlightenment and detachment from the world. Japanese samurai found in Zen a means of improving their combat readiness and fighting skills. Samurai who steeped themselves in Zen became indifferent to fear, discomfort, and the threat of death. Their focus, therefore, was defeating their foes, no matter the cost to themselves.

This Zen mindset was complemented by extensive training in specific forms of fighting, known as the martial arts. Each samurai warrior typically mastered at least one or two of these special fighting arts for use in battle. Using deadly weapons such as swords and spears was second-nature to the samurai, but they could also engage the enemy in unarmed, hand-to-hand combat. A number of the martial arts relied on using parts of a warrior's body, especially the hands and feet, as weapons.

The combination of having no fear and being exceptionally skilled fighters made the samurai feared and steadfast warriors.

LIVING BY THE SWORD

There is a traditional saying in Japan that "the sword is the soul of the samurai." While these warriors had several weapons at their

"The Great Buddha" was built during the Kamakura shogunate, beginning in 1252 CE. This massive statue—more than 13 meters (42 feet) tall—sits outside Kotuku-in temple in Kanagawa Prefecture.

disposal, the one they used most often was the curved-blade sword called a katana. By order of the *shogun*, samurai were the only class of people who were allowed to carry a sword in public.

Samurai also used a shorter sword called a wakizashi. Referred to as a "companion sword," the wakizashi was more often used for rituals such as seppuku, more commonly known to Westerners as hara-kiri.

Samurai started their training in sword fighting, called *kenjutsu*, at an early age. At first they used bamboo sticks as swords, so they did not hurt themselves or their training opponents. Only after lots of training and recognition by their teacher as being ready did they graduate to practicing with a sharp katana sword.

Japanese martial arts enthusiasts training in the ancient art of kenjutsu. A few of the ways of the samurai are still practiced today, especially when it comes to the martial arts.

DEATH BEFORE DISHONOR

The honorable method of taking one's own life practiced by samurai warriors was known as seppuku,
which means "self-disembowelment." The word hara-
kiri, meaning "belly-cutting," though widely known to
foreigners, is rarely used by the Japanese.

Seppuku evolved during the wars of the twelfth century
as a method of suicide used frequently by warriors who,
defeated in battle, chose to
avoid the dishonor of fall-
ing into the hands of the
enemy. Occasionally, a samurai performed seppuku
to demonstrate loyalty to
his lord by following him
in death, to protest against
some policy of a superior
or of the government, or
to atone for failure in his
duties. Being an extremely
painful and slow means
of suicide, it was favored
as an effective way to
demonstrate the courage,
self-control, and strong re-
solve of the samurai and to
prove sincerity of purpose.

*Japanese print showing a disgraced
general preparing to commit seppuku
after losing a battle.*

Making a traditional samurai sword was truly an art form. It took days, sometimes weeks, to create a weapon that was both strong and resilient, meaning able to withstand attack without damage. Samurai swords are formed from steel that is a combination of iron ore and carbon from charcoal. Extremely hot fires are used to pull the ore out of a special kind of sand. High heat is also applied when the carbon-filled ore chunks are folded, to make the material stronger, and when the sword blade is hammered into shape.

A Japanese sword maker in 1952 creating a samurai sword using the traditional method used for generations.

Once the sword has been hammered into the correct length and thickness, the blade is heated one more time, then dipped in cold water. This process is called quenching. Going from extreme heat to cold water makes the metal contract, meaning smaller or more compact. The contraction strengthens the steel, and also gives the katana its distinct curved edge.

Dressed to Kill

To protect themselves during armed battle, samurai warriors wore armor, complete with a helmet. Primitive quilted armor was often reinforced with small plates of hard material, such as bone, horn, horse hoofs, leather, or metal. Such scale armor originated in Asia and was worn by early samurai. Later, warriors used panels or smaller scales of metal, typically iron. The Japanese also used chain mail to a limited extent from the fourteenth century, though the rings in Japanese mail produced a more open construction than that found in Europe.

Samurai armor consisted of a breast plate covering the chest and abdomen, panels worn around the arms and legs, shoulder pads, and a paneled metal "skirt" that protected their mid-section. Curved metal panels topped with a wooden crest, which usually was shaped like animal horns, made up a samurai helmet. Metal strips hung from the sides of the helmet to protect the neck.

Samurai armor on display in a museum. Note the many different panels that made up the protective gear, and the horn-like pieces on either side of the helmet.

UNARMED BUT DANGEROUS

Samurai warriors were trained in armed and unarmed arts. In unarmed arts, opponents use their feet and hands to strike or wrestle with each other.

Jujitsu, meaning "gentle art," was a form of martial art and method of fighting evolved among the warrior class, or samurai, in Japan from about the seventeenth century. The term "gentle"

ARROW AND SPEAR

Kyudo, or archery, was used in early Japan for fishing and hunting. Later it became a military art. Samurai mostly shot their arrows while riding on horseback. The bow (*yumi*), made of wood and bamboo, was usually about 7.5 feet (2.3 meters) long. Bamboo arrows also were long, with a very sharp stone head, or tip.

Other weapons used by the samurai included two types of spear: the *yari* and the *naginata*. The *yari* featured a long, straight blade at the end, while the blade of the *naginata* was curved, like a katana blade. Some samurai were skilled at using a special fan called a *tessen*. The handle and ribs—the straight pieces that give the fan shape when opened—were made of iron. Wire might also be attached along the outer edge of the fan, to allow for better cutting moves.

describes the way in which samurai would not attack outright, but rather control an opponent's attack and use it against him. In its practice, jujitsu was anything but gentle. It involved hitting, kicking, kneeing, throwing, choking, and the use of certain weapons. Designed to complement a warrior's swordsmanship in combat, this style of fighting made use of few or no weapons. Instead, participants used holds, throws, and blows meant to stop opponents dead in their tracks.

Karate, which literally means "the art of empty hands," originated in Okinawa, Japan, many centuries ago. This martial art was based on combat techniques imported from China. Karate is a means of self-defense that uses striking, kicking, and blocking.

CHAPTER 3

NOTABLE BATTLES AND CONFLICTS

The first samurai protected vast lands owned by members of Japan's upper class. They engaged in fighting when there was a threat to their lord or his land-holdings. These threats could come from inside Japan or from foreign powers looking to overthrow the Japanese empire. Later, as members of the military class, samurai warriors were involved in battles because they were, essentially, Japan's army.

THE GEMPEI WAR

The Gempei War (1180–85) was the final struggle in Japan between the Taira and Minamoto clans that resulted in the establishment of the Kamakura shogunate. The Taira clan, who had dominated the Imperial government from 1160 to 1180, gained control of the strategic east coast of Japan, and by 1182 was ready to advance on the capital at Kyōto. The Taira leaders fled, taking with them the infant emperor Antoku. In the sea battle of Dannoura (1185) on the Inland Sea in western Japan, the Taira were finally defeated.

Although the Gempei War ended in 1185, a dispute between Minamoto Yoritomo and his brother Yoshitsune resulted in continued warfare until 1189, when Yoritomo finally destroyed the north-

A detail from a screen painting showing samurai on horseback approaching a battlefield during the Gempei War.

ern Fujiwara family, which had sheltered his rebellious brother. Three years later Yoritomo went to Kyōto and was appointed *shogun*, the highest honor that could be accorded a warrior.

THE MONGOL INVASIONS

The samurai of the Kamakura shogunate successfully repelled Mongol invasions in 1274 and in 1281. The Mongols were a group of people living in central Asia, in a vast highland region in what are now Mongolia and northern China. By the thirteenth century a confederation of nomadic Mongol tribes had become a powerful military force. Under the leadership of Genghis Khan and his successors, they established an empire that reached from what are now China and Korea in the east to eastern Europe and the shores of the Persian Gulf in the west.

In 1274, a Mongol army, under the command of Kublai Khan (Genghis's grandson), landed in Hakata Bay, on the Japanese island of Kyushu. A typhoon suddenly arose, destroying more than two hundred Mongol ships and the men on them. The survivors retreated to southern Korea.

In 1281, the Mongols tried to invade and conquer Japan again, attacking once more at Hakata Bay. Samurai forces had strengthened defenses along the coast of the bay. They also had built a huge stone wall inland around the bay, to keep opponents from gaining ground by land. Another typhoon destroyed most of the Mongol ships in the bay, including many Mongol fighters who had not

Artist's interpretation of the battle that raged in Hakata Bay as Mongol forces tried to invade Japan in 1281.

been able to land. Almost all of the remaining Mongol warriors were captured by Japanese forces.

Defending against both Mongol attacks took its toll on the Kamakura shogunate. The expense of defending Hakata Bay had bankrupted many landowners for whom the samurai worked. However, the Japanese people were very proud of the fighting abilities of the samurai. They also believed that the typhoons that destroyed their enemies during both invasion attempts were sent from the heavens, and that Japan was blessed by the gods.

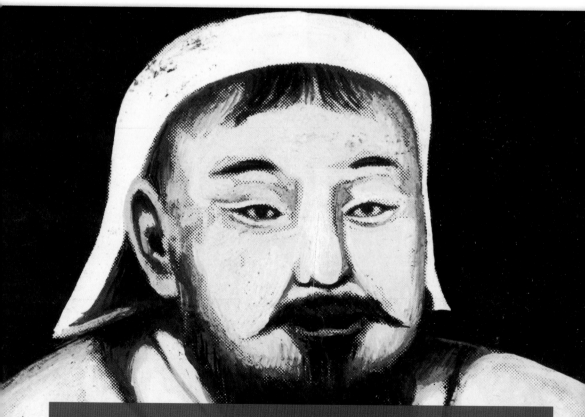

The infamous warrior Genghis Khan, pictured here, established the vast Mongol Empire in the thirteenth century. His grandson Kublai Khan made two disastrous attempts to invade Japan, in 1274 and 1281.

THE BATTLE AT NAGASHINO

In May of 1575, forces led by Takeda Katsuyori were traveling to the capital city of Kyoto; whoever controlled Kyoto controlled Japan. Standing in their way was a group of samurai loyal to Tokugawa Ieyasu, who were stationed at Nagashino castle. Takeda forces outnumbered the Tokugawa at Nagashino. It soon became obvious that reinforcements would be necessary to fight off the Takeda.

Tokugawa had an alliance, or agreement, with a neighboring warlord named Oda Nobunaga. A brilliant military mind, Oda had become famous for overthrowing the Ashikaga shogunate in 1573. In doing so, he ended a long period of internal strife by uniting half of Japan's provinces under his rule.

Statue of Oda Nobunaga at Kiyosu Castle. Nobunaga was a brilliant samurai warrior who helped bring modern warfare to Japan.

Oda was quick to seize on any promising new invention. He was the first of the Japanese warlords to organize units equipped with muskets. At Nagashino castle, Oda had his troops build a wooden stockade, or large fence, between the castle and the Takeda troops. Behind the stockade he positioned samurai armed with matchlock guns, which were an early version of today's rifle. He positioned the gunmen in three lines. That way, a line of warriors could fire on the enemy while those who had just fired could go to the back line and reload their weapons.

Takeda's army, which attacked on horseback using traditional samurai weapons, was no match for the guns of those inside the castle. After hours of fighting,

A man wearing samurai battle gear from the Endo period during a festival in Osaka. He is holding a matchlock rifle, used by warriors in the Battle of Nagashino.

THE ŌNIN WAR (1467–77)

The Ōnin War was a civil war in the central Kyōto region of Japan. The war originated in rivalry between Hosokawa Katsumoto, prime minister (1452–64) for the shogun Ashikaga Yoshimasa and Yamana Mochitoyo, whose families were powerful landowners in the western Honshu region. Ashikaga had declared that his brother Yoshimi would succeed him as shogun, but his wife wanted their son to become the next shogun. She turned to the Yamana family for help, starting a war between the two sides in 1467. Samurai loyal to each faction began a bloody battle that spread throughout the country. Local clans took sides in hopes of gaining more territory for themselves.

The war ended in a stalemate in 1477, with forces loyal to Yoshimi winning control of the government. However, fighting in the provinces continued for another one hundred years.

Portrait of shogun Yoshimasa, whose selection of a successor to the shogunate was at the heart of the famous Ōnin War.

nearly two-thirds of the Takeda warriors were dead, and the fighting was over.

The battle was important for two main reasons. First, it confirmed to samurai commanders that guns were extremely powerful weapons. Afterward, more and more samurai started using matchlocks in battle. Second, the battle led to the end of the Takeda and paved the way for the victorious Oda to lead Japan closer to unification.

CHAPTER 4

THE END OF THE SAMURAI

Under the Tokugawa shogunate (1603–1867), Japan enjoyed extraordinary peace and stability. Tokugawa Ieyasu and his successors built an elaborate system of controls over the daimyo, including limits on their military strength. The Tokugawa leaders cut back foreign trade, and the Japanese were forbidden to leave the country. The country entered a period of seclusion that lasted for more than two hundred years. Peace and isolationism, which meant the country did not deal with other nations, meant fewer conflicts—and less need for the samurai warrior class.

THE BEGINNING OF THE END

The seclusion of Japan ended in 1853 with the arrival of a United States naval fleet commanded by Commodore Matthew C. Perry. He had been instructed to open Japan to foreign trade and diplomatic contact. The Edo *bakufu*, recognizing US military superiority, signed a treaty of friendship with the United States during a second visit by Perry in 1854.

The Netherlands, Russia, Great Britain, and France followed the lead of the United States. By 1859 the *bakufu* had been pressured into signing a series of treaties that gave privileges to

Western powers at Japan's expense. Many Japanese regarded the surrender to the West as a national humiliation, and the *bakufu*'s authority declined rapidly. Demands for the expulsion of the foreigners and the restoration of political power to the emperor were supported by the court and two powerful daimyo domains—Satsuma and Choshu.

In 1867 the Tokugawa shogun was forced to give up power. Less than a year later a new government was established under the young emperor Mutsuhito, who took the reign name of Meiji ("enlightened government"). This transfer of power from the Tokugawa shogunate to the Meiji emperor is known as the Meiji Restoration. It is generally regarded as the beginning of Japan's modern era.

The new government wished to end the "unequal treaties" and catch up militarily with the Western countries. Their first task, however, was to create internal order. A centralized administration replaced the daimyo system. Many class distinctions were abolished. A conscript army was built up, replacing the samurai, or warrior class.

GOING OUT FIGHTING

During the 1870s the Imperial army quelled a number of rebellions by former samurai who objected to rapid modernization. In Chōshū, warriors revolted over government measures that deprived the samurai of their

Portrait of Japanese emperor Mutsuhito, by artist Uchida Kyuichi. His reign, known as the Meiji Restoration, saw Japan move from feudalism to an industrial society.

This image shows samurai, who objected to Japan's modernization, being captured and brought before leaders of the Imperial army.

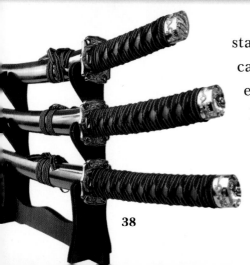

status and income. In Saga, samurai called for a foreign war to provide employment for their fading class. The last, and by far the greatest, revolt was the Satsuma rebellion of 1877, named for the region from which it sprang.

This uprising was led by the legendary samurai hero known as Saigō Takamori.

A leader in the overthrow of the Tokugawa shogunate, Saigō later rebelled against the weaknesses he saw in the Imperial government that he had helped to restore. He was deeply ashamed that the samurai had been so greatly dishonored through being replaced by the Imperial army. Making matters worse, other symbolic class distinctions, such as the hairstyle of samurai and the privilege of wearing swords, were abolished. Above all else, he seemed to resent the samurai's overall loss of military power.

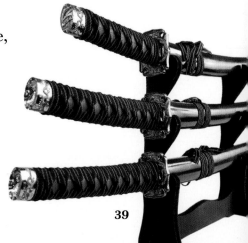

THE SIGNIFICANCE OF TOPKNOTS

When he had completed his training and come of age, usually between thirteen and fifteen, a young samurai would receive a new hairstyle called a *chomage*. His hair would be shaved in front, while the sides and back would be pulled into a special ponytail Westerners call a topknot.

The topknot could be difficult to wear under a helmet, so many warriors wore their hair down or straight and covered with a cloth while fighting in full armor. When not in battle, however, the topknot stayed on his head

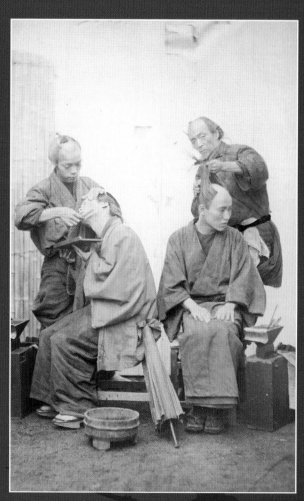

Japanese barbers in the late 1800s shaved young samurai and styled their hair into traditional topknots.

as a symbol of his status as a samurai. Several sources claim that when a warrior cut off his own topknot—or had it cut off by the enemy in battle—he was dishonored and lost his status in the warrior class.

In February 1877, Saigō led an army of his followers on a march toward Edo, which had been renamed Tokyo. Fighting started shortly thereafter, and the Satsuma rebellion was in full swing. During the summer, Saigō's troops suffered a series of disastrous defeats, and by September the situation was hopeless. With a few hundred men, he made one last stand on a hill overlooking the city of Kagoshima. Saigō was critically wounded in the battle. As had previously been arranged, in traditional samurai fashion, one of his faithful lieutenants took his life by beheading him.

The uprising in Satsuma lasted six months. When it was over, so was the last major challenge to the new imperial regime in Japan.

SAMURAI LEGACY

The spirit of the samurai warrior lives on in a number of ways in Japan. In modern times versions of the armed martial arts are practiced as sports. Katanas are no longer used in

Saigō Takamori, the rebel military leader during samurai uprisings in the late nineteenth century.

combat, but newly made swords and ancient examples are sought by museums and private collectors around the world.

Perhaps the most lasting contribution of the samurai lies in the Bushido code of conduct. The loyalty and honor exhibited by samurai warriors are two traits that are rooted in Japanese culture, as well as valued in other societies, to this day.

GLOSSARY

bakufu Term used to describe the rule of a Japanese military leader, meaning "tent government."

Bushido A code of conduct followed closely by the samurai.

crest A picture or shape worn on a knight's helmet.

daimyo An important local lord in the early days of Japan.

disembowel The act of injuring or removing one's internal organs.

domain The land that a ruler or government controls.

faction A group within a larger group that has different ideas and opinions than the main group.

filial Of or relating to a son or daughter.

indifferent Not interested in or concerned about something.

isolationism The belief that a country should not get involved with other countries.

katana A Japanese sword with a curved blade, which was the favorite weapon of the country's samurai warriors.

martial Of or relating to war or soldiers.

matchlock A type of early gun that was fired after a slow-burning match (fuse) made contact with gunpowder.

piety Devotion to a person or thing that is above one, including parents or other elders.

province Any one of the large parts that some countries are divided into.

reinforcements Something that encourages or strengthens another thing.

repel To stop something or turn it away.

shogunate The rule of military leaders in pre-modern Japan.

steadfast Very devoted and loyal, without the chance of changing.

stockade A line of tall posts that are set in the ground and used as a barrier to protect or defend a place.

topknot A cluster of hair worn at the top of the head.

typhoon A very large, destructive storm, similar to a hurricane.

uprising A usually violent effort by many people to change the government or leader of a country.

FOR FURTHER READING

Doeden, Matt. *Life as a Samurai: An Interactive History Adventure.*
Mankato, MN: Capstone Press, 2010.

Hepperman, Christine. *Samurai.* Minneapolis, MN: ABDO
Publishing Company, 2013.

Lee, Adrienne. *Legendary Warriors: Samurai.* Mankato, MN:
Capstone Press, 2013.

McLeese, Don. *Warriors Graphic Illustrated: Samurai.* Vero Beach, FL:
Rourke Educational Media, 2011.

Owen, Ruth. *The World of the Samurai Warrior.* New York, NY:
Bearport Publishing (Ruby Tuesday Books), 2014.

Riggs, Kate. *Samurai.* Mankato, MN: Creative Education, 2011.

Turner, Pamela S. *Samurai Rising: The Epic Life of Minamoto
Yoshitsune.* Watertown, MA: Charlesbridge Publishing, 2016.

Yei, Theodora Ozaki. *Warriors of Old Japan.* San Diego, CA:
Didactic Press, 2014.

WEBSITES

Because of the changing nature of internet links, Rosen Publishing has developed an online list of websites related to the subject of this book. This site is updated regularly. Please use this link to access the list:

http://www.rosenlinks.com/WAW/samurai

INDEX